My First Animal Library

Iguanas

by Mari Schuh

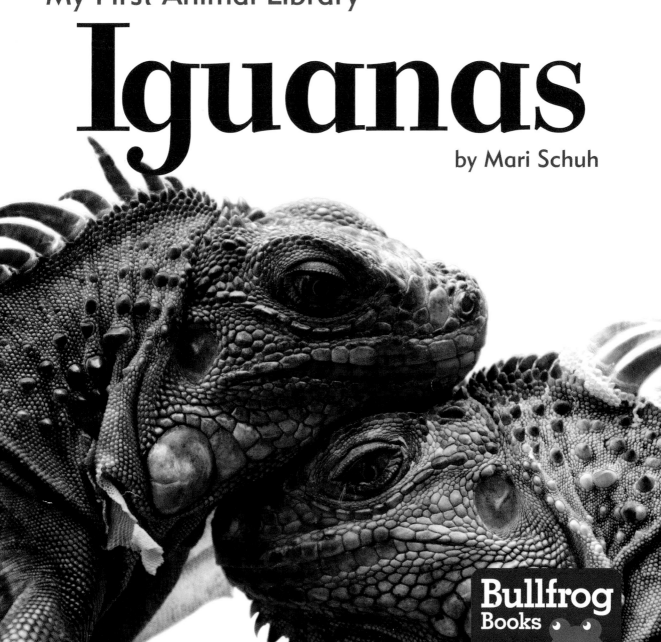

Bullfrog Books

Ideas for Parents and Teachers

Bullfrog Books let children practice reading informational text at the earliest reading levels. Repetition, familiar words, and photo labels support early readers.

Before Reading

- Discuss the cover photo. What does it tell them?
- Look at the picture glossary together. Read and discuss the words.

Read the Book

- "Walk" through the book and look at the photos. Let the child ask questions. Point out the photo labels.
- Read the book to the child, or have him or her read independently.

After Reading

- Prompt the child to think more. Ask: How does the iguana's green color keep it safe? What is your favorite hiding place? What colors can you wear to hide in that place?

Dedicated to Fairmont Area Schools —MS

Bullfrog Books are published by Jump!
5357 Penn Avenue South
Minneapolis, MN 55419
www.jumplibrary.com

Library of Congress Cataloging-in-Publication Data
Schuh, Mari C., 1975- author.
  Iguanas / by Mari Schuh.
    pages cm.—(My first animal library)
  Summary: "This photo-illustrated book for early readers tells the story of a rain forest iguana searching for food and escaping a hawk"—Provided by publisher.
  Audience: 5-8.
  Audience: Grade K to 3.
  Includes bibliographical references and index.
  ISBN 978-1-62031-110-3 (hardcover)
  ISBN 978-1-62496-177-9 (ebook)
  1. Iguanas—Juvenile literature. I. Title.
  QL666.L25S37 2015
  597.95'42—dc23
                                    2013042376

Editor: Wendy Dieker
Series Designer: Ellen Huber
Book Designer: Lindaanne Donohoe
Photo Researcher: Kurtis Kinneman

Photo Credits: All photos by Shutterstock except: Alamy, 8–9; iStockphoto, cover, 11, 12, 17, 23br; SuperStock, 14–15, 16

Printed in the United States of America at Corporate Graphics, North Mankato, Minnesota.
6-2014
10 9 8 7 6 5 4 3 2 1

Table of Contents

Green Lizards

Look high in the trees.
What do you see? An iguana!

claw

Iguanas live in
the rain forest.

Sharp claws
help them
climb trees.

A long tail helps
them balance.

An iguana looks
for plants to eat.

He finds flowers.

He finds leaves.

He eats fruit, too.

Look out! A hawk!

The iguana stays still.
Maybe the hawk
won't see him.

Look at his green scales.
They cover his body.
His color helps him hide.

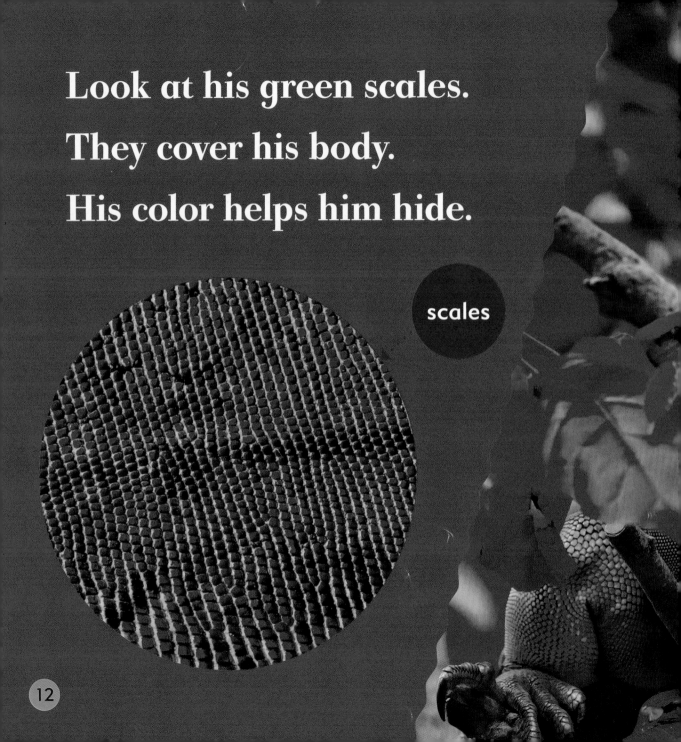

scales

Time to get away.

Splash!

He jumps into
the river.

He swims. He dives.

He is safe.

17

The iguana finds
a sunny spot.

The sun
warms him.

Now he is warm and dry.

Parts of an Iguana

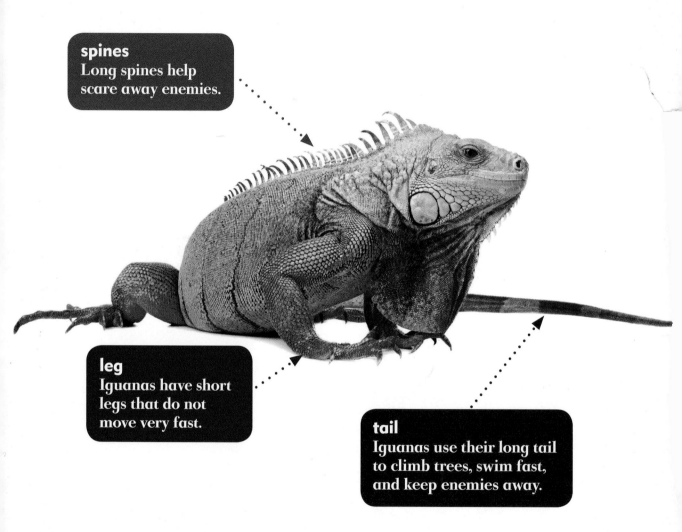

spines
Long spines help scare away enemies.

leg
Iguanas have short legs that do not move very fast.

tail
Iguanas use their long tail to climb trees, swim fast, and keep enemies away.

Picture Glossary

claw
A hard, curved nail on an iguana's foot.

rain forest
A thick area of trees where a lot of rain falls.

hawk
A large bird with a hooked beak that eats other animals.

scales
Tiny, thin parts that cover an iguana's body.

Index

To Learn More

Learning more is as easy as 1, 2, 3.

1) Go to www.factsurfer.com

2) Enter "iguanas" into the search box.

3) Click the "Surf" button to see a list of websites.

With factsurfer.com, finding more information is just a click away.

24